P9-DWY-588

Feltcraft

Petra Berger

Feltcraft

Making Dolls, Gifts and Toys

Floris Books

Translated by Polly Lawson

Photographs by Wim Steenkamp and Thomas Berger
Illustrations by Ronald Heuninck

First published in Dutch under the title *Spelen met vilt*
by Christofoor Publishers in 1994
First published in English in 1994 by Floris Books
Fifth impression 2001

© Christofoor, Zeist 1994
This translation © Floris Books 1994
All rights reserved. No part of this book may
be reproduced in any form without the prior permission of
Floris Books, 15 Harrison Gardens, Edinburgh.

British Library CIP Data available

ISBN 0-86315-190-6

Printed in Belgium

Contents

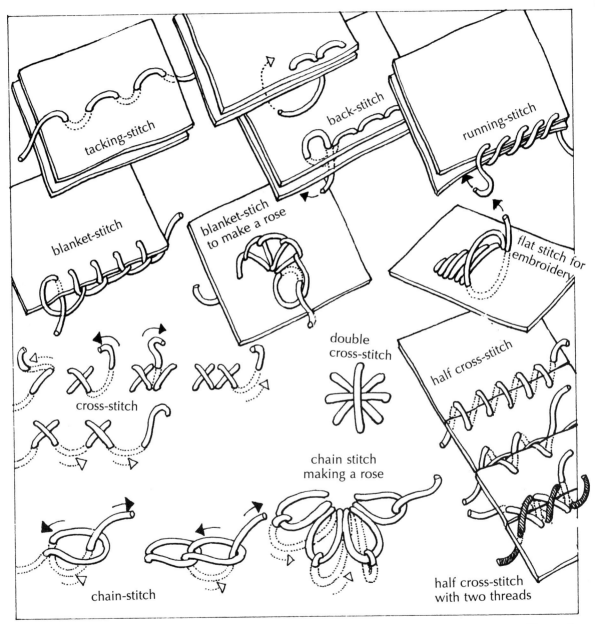

tacking-stitch

back-stitch

running-stitch

blanket-stitch

blanket-stich
to make a rose

flat stitch for
embroidery

cross-stitch

double
cross-stitch

half cross-stitch

chain stitch
making a rose

chain-stitch

half cross-stitch
with two threads

6

Figure 1.

Introduction

Felt is a splendid material for working with:
— children can work with it easily
— it is strong and firm
— it can be cut out easily into different shapes
— it does not fray.

There are different kinds of felt on the market: from synthetic and half-synthetic to pure woollen felt. Generally the synthetic felt is not satisfactory because it is very thin and the threads are too loosely woven, so while it is being sewn it can easily come apart.

Pure woollen felt, available in a variety of colours, is quite expensive. You normally need only small pieces because the things in this book are generally small.

When you are making dolls choose the colours with care. Try to give each doll its own character by using the right colour and avoid simply standardizing the colour scheme.

When making objects for young children try to make a true image: so for example, do not hang elephants or cars on a mobile because they do not belong there, but birds, butterflies and fairies do.

The objects in this book are mostly small. This applies also to the separate parts of the patterns. It is better not to use pins as this causes the material to rumple and spoil the shape.

Sometimes it is better to tack two layers of felt together before cutting them out together.

The patterns throughout this book are drawn to full scale. It is best to cut them out generously as they can easily be trimmed.

Embroidery stitches

Figure 1 shows a number of stitches which can be used with felt. The simple stitches are usually used to sew pieces together.

Tacking-stitch is used frequently for gathering and for embellishing tapestry, as well as for tacking.

In general *back-stitch* is used to sew two parts together. Sometimes you can use *blanket-stitch* or *button-hole stitch* for this but that causes a little edge to stand up (see the little dog with the finger-puppets on page 29). For the scissor case (page 83) this is used for decoration.

Cross-stitch is really a kind of back-stitch. *Half cross-stitch* is used particularly in this book for sewing the balls together (see page 73). Of course cross-stitch is also used a lot for embellishing. Other stitches in Figure 1 are always used for embellishing, as for example in the tapestries (pages 63-67).

Making the hair

The simplest hairstyle is made from thinly teased unspun wool or carded fleece. Drape the wool over the head. On dolls made of wood glue the wool to the head, but on dolls made of soft fabric sew it on.

With three very thin strands of wool you can also make a plait.

With thin knitting wool you can make many more variations. The woman in Figure 38 has hair with a parting. To achieve this, wind the thin knitting wool twenty or thirty times round two or three of your fingers. Take the wool off your fingers and run a tacking-thread in and out through the strands a few times to bind them together. Glue the hair onto the wooden head and cut through the loops. You will need to sew the hair onto a head made of soft fabric.

For the *mop hairstyle* in Figure 44 first tack the yarns firmly together, but then pull the tacking threads hard together so that from one point the hair stands up in all directions.

For the *curly-head* sew separate loops, each loop being sewn on with a little stitch, after which the next loop is made.

The *embroidering* of the hair is done with stitches going from the crown downwards.

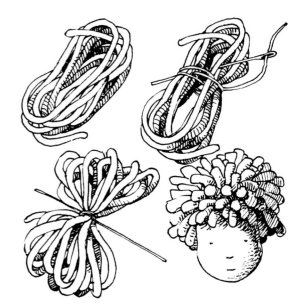

∧ *Figure 2.*

∨ *Figure 3.*

8

Wooden standing dolls

You can buy wooden dolls in many sizes and shapes, either with a cylindrical body or with one which widens out towards the bottom. The larger wooden dolls sometimes have a hole in the base so that they can be used as finger-puppets.

When you buy the dolls check carefully that the heads are smooth and round and that they are not pitted.

If you are unable to buy a wooden doll you can make one out of a cork and a large wooden bead.

Pare round the top of the cork to make a round sloping side (Figure 3).

Make a hole in the top of the cork with a wooden skewer or cocktail stick. Cover the end of the skewer with glue and stick it firmly into the hole.

Then glue a large wooden bead onto the skewer. Cut off the remainder of the skewer.

To finish, wrap a thick thread around the neck, leaving a neck of roughly ¼" (5 mm) (Figure 3).

Gnomes

Materials
Wooden dolls 2¼" and 3" (6 and 7 cm) high
Pieces of felt
Unspun wool or carded fleece

Method
Clothe the body by gluing a piece of felt onto it and sew up the back seam. Trim the felt.

The pattern of the *jacket* in Figure 5 shows the measurements for both the gnomes. Lay the

Figure 4.

9

jacket round the body and secure it at the neck with a few stitches.

Before you cut out the *cap* of the pattern in Figure 5 check the exact circumference of the head as this can vary.

Cut out the cap from a double piece of felt, sew up the back seam and glue the cap onto the wooden head.

Now take a little tuft of unspun wool or carded fleece and tease it well out before gluing it onto the head as hair and beard.

If you want, you can draw a face with a coloured pencil.

A royal family

Materials
Wooden dolls, 2", 2½" and 3" (5, 6 and 7 cm) high
Pieces of felt
Unspun wool, carded fleece or knitting wool

Method
Clothe the bodies with a felt robe as was described under *gnomes*.

Figure 7 shows that the king's robe is embroidered while the queen's is embellished with little beads. Take the measurements of the clothes, cut them out and embroider them before gluing the felt onto the body and sewing it up the back.

Figure 5. Pattern for wooden gnomes.

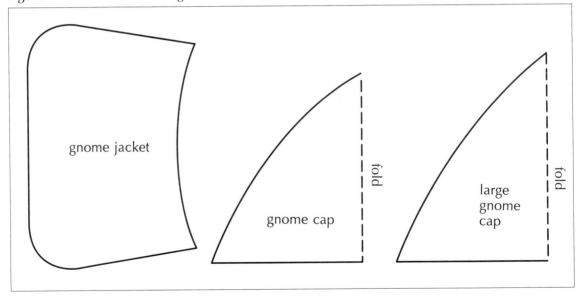

gnome jacket

gnome cap

fold

large gnome cap

fold

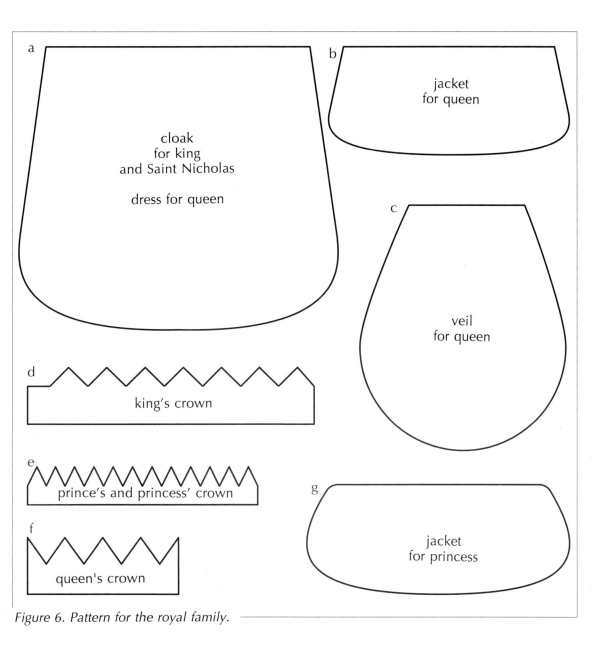

a cloak
for king
and Saint Nicholas

dress for queen

b jacket
for queen

c veil
for queen

d king's crown

e prince's and princess' crown

f queen's crown

g jacket
for princess

Figure 6. Pattern for the royal family.

11

Figure 7.

Cloak and jackets

Figure 6 shows the patterns for the king's cloak and the jackets for the rest of the family. Each one is differently made and embroidered. The princess's coat is 3¼" x 1¼" (8 x 3.2 cm). Cut out the edges with pinking scissors.

Cut out each item of clothing and embroider it. Gather the top edge and secure it round the doll's neck.

Finishing off

Make the dolls' hair and the king's white beard from unspun wool or carded fleece (see page 8) and glue them on. The princess has a plait of yellow teased fleece (or thick knitting wool).

Gather the top edge of the queen's *veil*, then glue it to the back of her head. Finally cut out the crowns and stitch them to the hair.

Saint Nicholas

Materials
Wooden dolls 2¾" and 2" (7 and 5 cm) high
Pieces of felt and a scrap of lace
Unspun wool or carded fleece
Stiff card

Method
Make St Nicholas in the same way as the king on (see the pattern in Figure 6). His robe is about ½" (1 cm) shorter and has a lace bottom hem. Glue a red strip of felt behind the lace. When you sew on the gold trimmings remember that the inside of the cloak is visible so you must not let the stitches go right through the felt (Figure 8).

Figure 8.

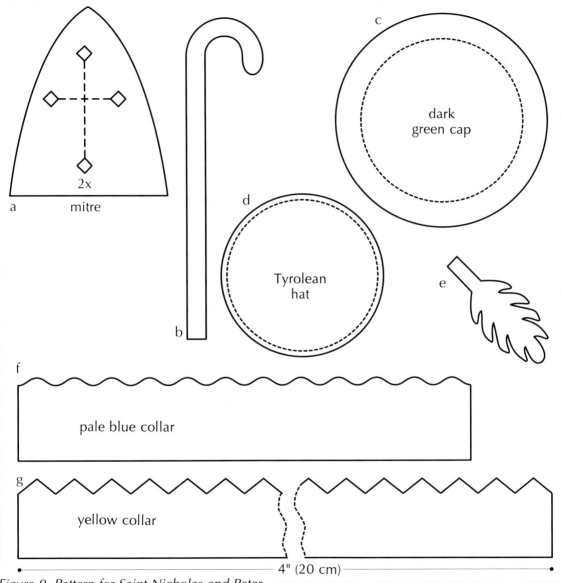

a   2x   mitre

b

c   dark green cap

d   Tyrolean hat

e

f   pale blue collar

g   yellow collar

4" (20 cm)

Figure 9. Pattern for Saint Nicholas and Peter.

13

St Nicholas has an embroidered mitre (see pattern in Figure 9a). Cut the staff out of felt and card. Glue the card onto the back of the felt.

Peter

In the Netherlands Saint Nicholas has one or more companion, Peter. Here is a pattern for a large Peter and a small one.

Blacken the wooden dolls' heads with poster-paint or Indian ink. For the clothes make tubes out of the pieces of felt. For the big Peter you will need a piece of felt about 3½" x 1½" (9 x 4 cm); and for the little Peter 2¾" x 1¼" (7 x 3.5 cm). In both cases gather the tube in at the top and secure it round the neck. The clothes are not glued to the wooden bodies.

Cut out the *collar*, gather it in at the top and secure it to the neck in the same way.

Each Peter has a different head-covering. For the big Peter gather the bonnet along the edge, draw it in round the head and secure. Little Peter has a Tyrolean hat: cut out a round piece of felt, gather it along the edge and draw the thread in to the circumference of the head.

v *Figure 10.*   *Figure 11.* >

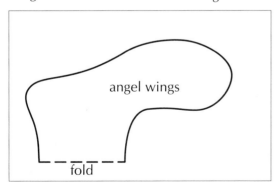

Little angel

Materials
Wooden doll 2¾" (7 cm) high
Pieces of felt
Little beads
Carded fleece
Gold foil

Method
Clothe the body with a piece of white felt.

Trim the bottom of the angel's dress with a thin strip of felt or some beads.

Cut out the wings (Figure 10). Decorate them either with little beads or with different coloured pieces of felt with matching designs cut into them. These pieces can be glued onto the wings. Use teased wool for the hair. You can give the angel a hair-band and a little star.

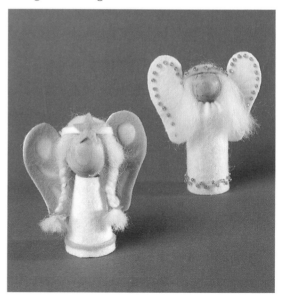

Mother with baby

Materials
Wooden dolls 2¼" & 1¼" (6 & 3 cm) in length
Pieces of felt
Pipe-cleaners
Unvarnished wooden beads about ¼" (7 mm)
    diameter
Walnut shells

The Mother
Glue a piece of felt onto the larger wooden doll's body. Sew up the back seam and trim the felt.

Take a piece of pipe-cleaner about 2½" (6–7 cm) long and stick beads onto each end to make hands. Then cut out the coat (Figure 13a)

Figure 12.

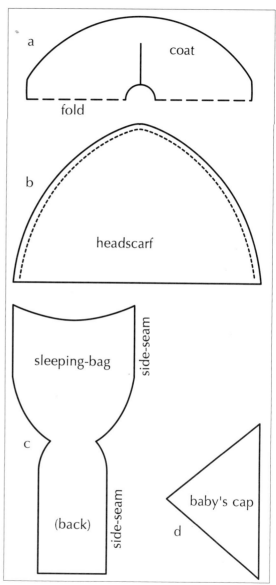

a   coat
fold

b   headscarf

c   sleeping-bag   side-seam

(back)   side-seam

d   baby's cap

Figure 13. Pattern for mother with baby.

and drape it round the doll's neck so that the opening is at the back. Lay the doll face down and put the pipe-cleaner arms over its back. Then sew up the back seam of the coat thus securing the arms.

Now cut out the headscarf (Figure 13b) and embroider the front with a woollen or cotton thread. Gather in the two bottom edges of the headscarf and glue onto the head.

The baby
Glue a little piece of felt round the body and a strip of felt round the neck for a collar. Cut out the cap (Figure 13d), glue it onto the head and secure with a few stitches. If you wish, you can give the baby some hair with some strands of wool.

The cradle
Cut out the sleeping-bag (Figure 13c), lay the baby on the wide half, and fold the narrow half back over the body. Bring the sides up around the baby and sew up the side seams. Take the baby out of the sleeping-bag and glue the bottom of the bag into the inside of half a walnut shell. Make sure you can still slip the baby in and out easily.

Hazelnut children

Materials
Hazelnuts
Unvarnished wooden beads with a diameter of ½"–⅝" (12–15 mm)
Pieces of felt
Unspun wool

Method
Wipe the hazelnuts clean and if necessary scrape the bottoms flat so that the children will not fall over. Glue a bead onto the top of each hazelnut for a head. Make sure the hole in the bead runs from top to bottom.

Take a tiny bit of unspun wool or some woollen yarn for the hair and glue this onto the head.

Cut out a piece of felt 1" (2.5 cm) wide and 2" (5–6 cm) long (depending on the size of the bead) and glue it to the head as a headscarf or bonnet. Tie it up at the neck with a piece of string (Figure 14).

First trim the bottom of the felt and then glue it securely onto the hazelnut. If you wish you can draw the eyes and mouth with a coloured pencil.

Figure 14.

Felt Dolls

Basic Model

Materials
White, pink or brown knitted cotton
Unspun wool
Pieces of felt
Thread
Thin card

The head
Take a piece of knitted cotton about 3" x 3" (8 x 8 cm). Make a little ball unspun wool about ¾" (2 cm) in diameter and lay it in the middle of the cotton. Wrap the cotton round the ball of wool and tie it round the neck (Figure 15b).

Figure 15.

Make sure that the head has as few creases as possible on one side, and use this side for the face. Trim the excess cotton straight across about 1" (2.5 cm) under the tie.

Later, once the doll is finished, you can carefully embroider the face. In order to get the eyes and mouth in the right place stick pins with coloured heads into the right places first.

The body
For the body of, for example, the flower children and the finger-puppets you will need a tube of felt. Vary the length and width of the body according to the doll.

Take a square piece of felt and sew two opposite sides together as shown in Figure 15c. Now gather in one of the open ends to make a neck. Insert the head into this gathered end of the tube, draw in the thread and sew the neck firmly into the tube (Figure 15d).

The doll should now be able to stand but if you stuff the tube with wool it will be firmer. You can also sew a round piece of felt of the same colour across the base. Now the basic form of the doll is finished.

The doll will stand better if you cut out a round piece of cardboard and stick it onto the felt base. Make the cardboard roughly ¹/₁₆" (2 mm) smaller than the felt base.

Figure 16.

Gnomes

Materials
Pieces of felt
Unspun wool or carded fleece

Method
Cut out the gnome's coat (Figure 17). Sew up the seam of the hood and run a gathering thread through at the place marked *gather*. Stuff a tuft of well-teased wool into the coat, draw in the thread and either tie it firmly at the front or sew up the coat. To make a beard draw out a little bit of the wool from the head or sew on a bit of wool. You can also tease out wool round the face.

Trim the wool at the bottom to make a flat base, so that the gnome can stand. Using the same proportions but changing the lengths shown in the pattern, you will be able to make different sized standing gnomes. Make sure that the heads do not become too small.

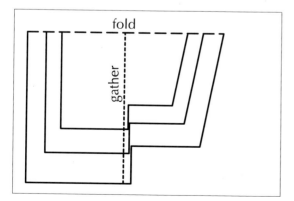

Figure 17.

Woollen dolls

Materials
Thick knitting wool of different colours
Threads of the same colours as the wool
Threads of contrasting colours
Stiff card

Method
The dolls shown in Figure 20 vary in length between 2¼" and 3¼" (6 and 8 cm). For the arms wind the knitting wool round a piece of card about 2¼" (6 cm) long (the width is not important). Depending on the thickness of the wool about twenty turns should do.

Tie up the ends with some thread of the same colour (Figure 18b). These will eventually

Figure 18.

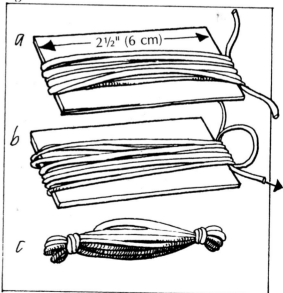

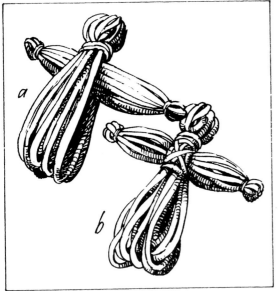

∧ *Figure 19.*   ∨ *Figure 20.*

be little round hands. Take the wool right off the card and tie it up at the wrists — about ½" (1 cm) from the ends (Figure 18c).

The head and the body are made using one piece of card. Take a piece of card about 2¾" (7 cm) long and wind the knitting wool round it about forty times, again depending on the thickness of the wool. Tie up one end of the yarn, where the head will be, and take the wool off the card. Now tie up the head at the neck about ¾" (2 cm) from the top (Figure 19a).

Now thrust the arms through the loop of the chest and then tie in the waist (Figure 19b).

Pull the waist up a bit so that the arms sit tight. You can also secure the arms more firmly by criss-crossing the thread over the chest.

If you are going to make a doll with a skirt you must cut open the loops at the bottom. If you wish to make legs then divide the loops into two equal parts and finish off as for the hands.

You can dress the dolls by giving them a conical cap of felt, a belt, a scarf or an apron.

Variation
If you wish, you can cut open the hands and feet like the doll in the middle in Figure 20. This makes a kind of brush.

Flower children

Materials
Pieces of felt
Pink or white knitted cotton
Unspun wool
Carded wool or fairy-tale wool
Pipe-cleaners
Thread

General method
For the head see the description on page 17. Vary the length and width of the body according to the kind of flower child.

The doll will stand as it is, but you can also fill the tube with wool and sew a round piece of felt of the same colour across the base, first sticking a round piece of card onto the bottom of the base. The card should be $^1/_{16}$" (2 mm) smaller than the round piece of felt. Flower children which carry flowers are inclined to topple over, so it is a good idea to sew in a marble or a pebble as a stabilizing weight.

This completes the basic construction of the flower children. The details for each specific flower follow.

The crocus

For the body take a piece of felt 2¼" x 2¼" (6 x 6 cm). For the collar take a piece of lilac-coloured felt 4" x 1½" (10 x 3.5 cm), and cut it out as in Figure 22a. Gather in the top edge and sew the collar round the neck.

Do the same for the crocus's cap. Gather the felt in a little at the place indicated so that the

Figure 21.

Figure 22. Pattern for crocus.

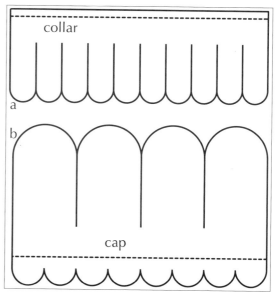

cap sits neatly on the head, but first give the flower child some hair of a suitable colour (fairy-tale wool for example). Secure the cap onto the head with a few stitches and then secure the tops of the petals, drawing together the ones which lie opposite each other.

The snowdrop
The snowdrop's body is 2¼" (6 cm) high and 2¾" (7 cm) wide. Cut out the collar (Figure 23a), gather it in and sew it onto the body.

The snowdrop's bonnet consists of three separate white petals (Figure 23b) sewn onto the top of a little light-green felt stalk (Figure 23c). First give the flower child's head some white woollen hair, then sew on the bonnet with a few stitches.

The snowdrop holds a separate flower which

Figure 23. Pattern for snowdrop.

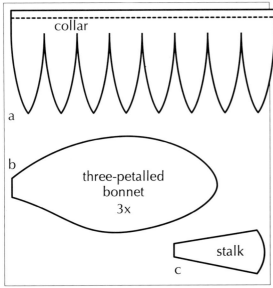

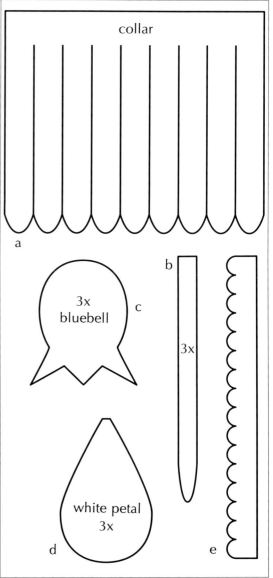

Figure 24. Pattern for bluebell and snowdrop.

consists of a green stalk with three separate white petals (Figure 24d). The piece of felt for the stalk is 5" x ½" (12½ x 1½ cm) rolled lengthwise round a pipe-cleaner and secured to it. The petals can then be sewn on.

The bluebell

The bluebell's body is 2¾" (7 cm) high and 2¼" (6 cm) wide. Cut out the collar (Figure 24a), gather it in and sew it onto the neck.

The bluebell wears a kind of petal hair-band of blue felt (Figures 21 left, 24e). To make the stalk for the separate flower follow the same procedure as described under the *snowdrop*. The bluebell then has three extra petals (Figure 24c) which must be sewn together and then secured to the stalk.

The tulip

The tulip's body is 2¼" (5.5 cm) high and 4" (10 cm) wide. Cut out the collar (Figure 25a), gather it in and sew it onto the body.

The tulip-child has a bonnet of six separate petals (Figure 25b). Sew the first two petals onto the side of the head. Then gather the remaining four petals in a little at the bottom, before sewing them onto the head overlapping each other (Figure 25c). Give the tulip some rose-coloured hair.

The daffodil

The daffodil's body is about 2" (5 cm) high and 4" (10 cm) wide. Cut out the collar (Figure 26a), gather it and sew it onto the body.

The daffodil's bonnet consists of two parts. First sew the gathered yellow wreath of petals

Figure 25. Pattern for tulip.

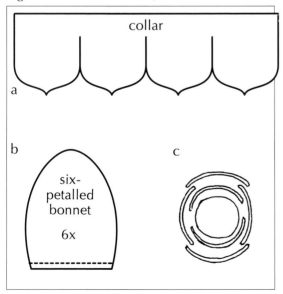

Figure 26. Pattern for daffodil.

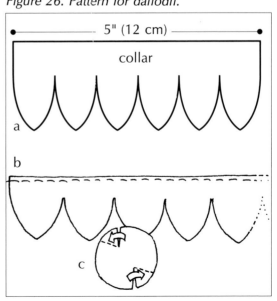

Figure 27.

onto the head. Next cut out a circle of dark yellow felt to make the heart of the flower. Make cuts into the opposite sides of the circle as in Figure 26c and sew up the inside as in the drawing so that it stands up as a dome. Sew the heart onto the crown of the head.

Blossom-fairies

Materials
Pieces of felt
Pink knitted cotton
Unspun wool
Carded fleece in various colours
Two unvarnished wooden beads, diameter ¼"
(5 mm)
Length of pipe-cleaner
Piece of thin card
Glue

Method
Follow the description on page 17 for the head.

Now make the gown. Choose soft colours to match the blossoms: white, pink, pale yellow and pale green.

Fold the piece of felt in half and cut out the pattern of Figure 29. Open the gown and cut the opening for the neck.

Push the head through the opening in the gown. Sew up the back seam of the neck-opening and secure the neck firmly to the gown (Figure 28).

To make the arms take about 3¼" (8 cm) of pipe-cleaner and insert it into the open sleeves of the gown. Now sew up the sleeves to secure the pipe-cleaner which should now stick out a

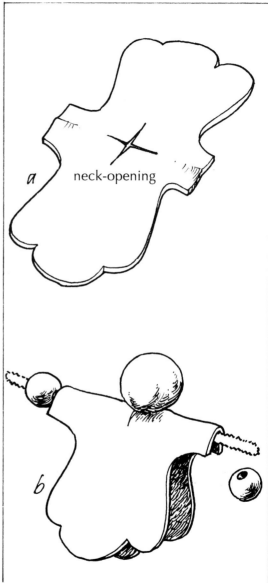

a   neck-opening

b

Figure 28.

bit from the sleeves. Apply a little glue to the ends of the pipe-cleaner and fix on the beads. As soon as the glue is dry any surplus pipe-cleaner can be cut off.

Tease out a little bit of carded fleece or unspun wool and sew it firmly onto the head together with a felt hair-band.

You can also fix a thread onto the top of the head in order to hang up the blossom-child. Do not use too short a thread: it can always be shortened afterwards. Hang the blossom-child among attractive branches (Figure 27).

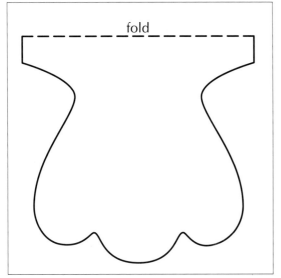

Figure 29. Pattern for blossom-fairy.

Finger-puppets

Materials
Pieces of felt
Unspun wool
Knitted cotton in various colours
Darning wool in various colours
Beads with a diameter or 1¼" (32 mm)
Small beads

Method
Finger-puppets must not only be able to stand, they must also fit onto fingers, so that they can act out stories. Children also love to play with them.

The total height of the finger-puppets is about 3¼" (8 cm); the head has a diameter of about ¾" (2 cm).

Follow the description on page 17 for the head. Make the body from a rectangular piece of felt 3" x 2¼" (7.5 x 6 cm). Sew the back seams together to make a tube (Figure 15c on page 17) Gather in the neck as shown, insert the head and secure it.

Dressing the finger-puppets
Figure 30 shows how the finger-puppets can be dressed differently. You may wish to invent your own variations.

African doll with plaits
Take a piece of felt 3½" x 2¼" (9 x 5.5 cm) for the coat. Fold over ½" (1 cm) of the top of the coat to make a collar. Trim round the corners. Sew the hands onto the coat (Figure 30). Place the coat firmly round the doll's neck and sew it on securely a bit lower down at the front.

Figure 30.

Secure the headscarf (Figure 31a) onto the head around the face, with the point at the back sewn onto the doll's back.

Make the plaits out of black darning wool. Tie the ends together and sew them onto the headscarf on the head. Embroider a fringe over the forehead. Give the doll a necklace of beads.

A little man with a hat

This doll wears a jacket which consists of two large sleeves only. Two hands are sewn onto these. The top edge of the sleeves is sewn onto the tube-body along the whole length, from one wrist to the other.

Cut out the tie (Figure 31e) and secure it with a few stitches. Use light-coloured darning wool to embroider hair from the crown of the head downwards.

The hat consists of three parts: a piece of felt 2½" x 1" (6.5 x 2.5 cm) and the two round pieces (Figure 31d). Cut out the parts of the hat, sew them together and secure them to the head.

Woman with a bun

This woman has an apron sewn onto her body. For the arms take a piece of felt 3½" x ¾" (9 x 2 cm). Fold the piece in half to 3½" x ³⁄₈" (9 x 1 cm), insert a pipe-cleaner into it and sew up the long seam. Then secure the hands in the sleeves and fasten the arms onto the back of the tube-body. Cut out the collar and sew it on (Patterns are in Figures 32a–d).

Embroider the hair from the crown of the head downwards.

For the bun twist a length of woollen yarn round your finger thirty or forty times (depending on the thickness of the wool). Remove the

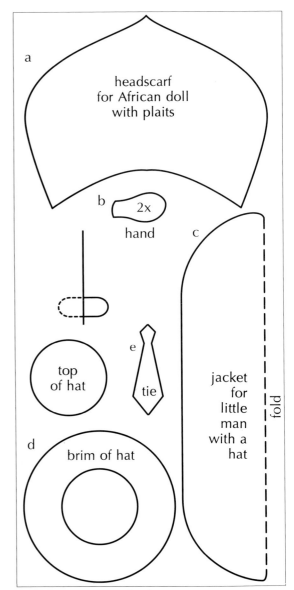

Figure 31. Pattern for finger-puppets.

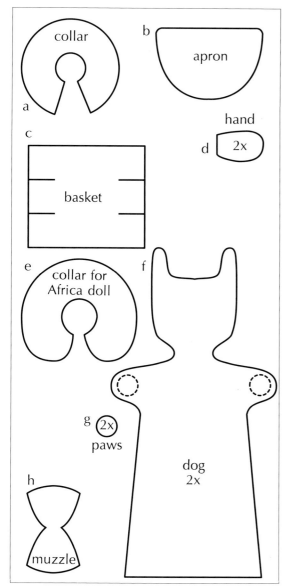

Figure 32. Pattern for finger-puppets.

wool from your finger, twist it into a bun and secure it to the back of the head with a few large stitches. Finally make the basket for her to hold.

African doll

This doll is made in a similar way to the *woman with a bun* but with this one the collar is quite a bit bigger (Figure 32e), there are big buttons on the dress and the hands are beads sewn onto the sleeves.

Make the hair by embroidering large loops, taking the needle back through the loop each time to secure it.

Little dog

The pattern of the little dog has an identical front and back, and a separate muzzle.

Cut out the pattern of Figure 32f and sew the two pieces together, filling the head with wool.

Now sew the muzzle together, stuff it with wool and sew it onto the front of the head.

Finish off the dog by giving him two beads for eyes (Figure 32g) and sewing two little circles onto his paws. Embroider the mouth on the muzzle.

Walking dolls

Materials
Pieces of felt
Unspun wool
Knitted cotton for the head and hands
Knitting wool
Pipe-cleaner

Method
Make a round head with a diameter of about 1¼" (3 cm) from unspun wool and a piece of knitted cotton. See page 17 for method.

As can be seen in Figure 34 you can make these dolls to walk. They consist of two parts: the upper body and the lower body, the latter being sewn to the former at the back. Both the man and the woman wear trousers; the woman wears hers under her dress.

For the arms and hands take a pipe-cleaner, doubling the two ends back a short way leaving the length of the pipe-cleaner at about 5" (12.5 cm). Wrap some teased unspun wool thinly round the pipe-cleaner and tie a piece of knitted cotton round both ends to make the hands.

The patterns in Figure 33 are for a pair of trousers with baggy legs, and for slippers or boots. Figure 35 has patterns for a dress for the woman, a jacket for the man, a headscarf, and a ponted hat.

Cut out the various parts of the pattern. Push the head through the neck-opening into the jacket or dress and sew it up.

Open out the jacket or dress and lay the arms inside it making sure that the hands stick out.

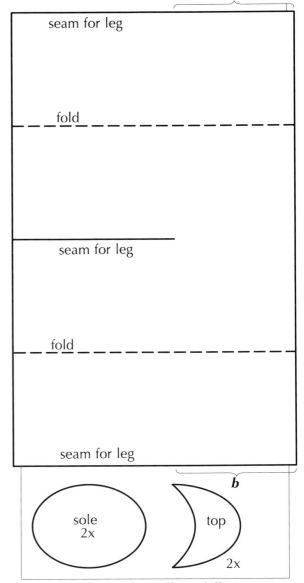

Figure 33. Pattern for walking dolls.

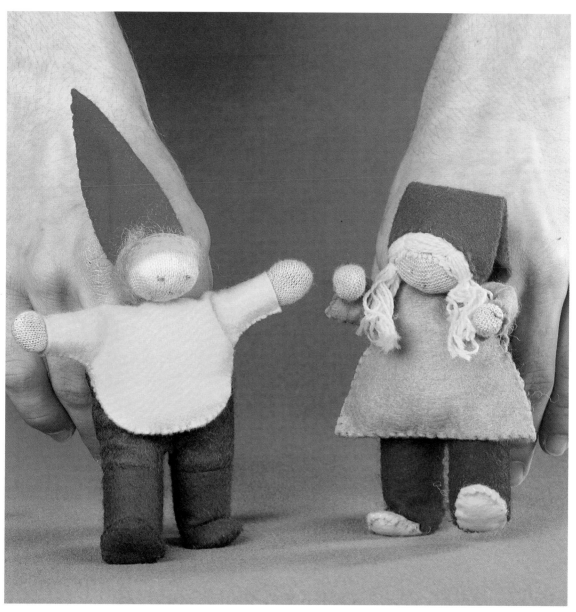

Figure 34.

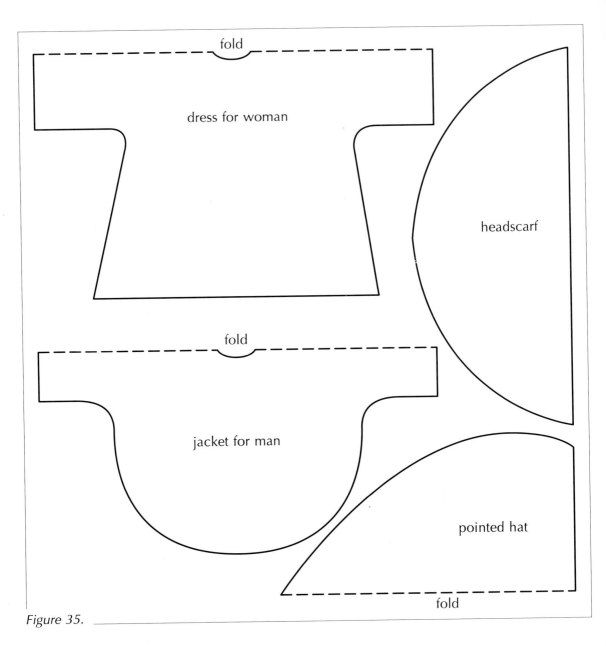

Figure 35.

32

Sew up the seams of the jacket almost completely but leave a little hole so that you can fill it loosely with wool. Then sew up the hole. This completes the upper body.

Cut out the trousers and sew them up so that side *a* is sewn to side *b*.

The man in Figure 34 has boots (you will need a piece 2½" x 1¼", 6.2 x 3.2 cm) and the woman has a pair of slippers. The procedure for the two of them is the same. Sew the tops of the man's boots to his trousers. Then sew up the soles and uppers of the boots and the slippers and stuff the tips of the footwear before sewing them onto the bottom of the trouser-legs. Sew the front of the trousers onto the waist underneath the jacket or dress. Leave the top of the trousers open and the back so that you can put two fingers in to the trouser-legs.

Finish off the dolls by giving them a hat or a headscarf — the man can have hair from teased wool, and the woman long hair from thin yellow knitting-wool. If you wish you can embroider the eyes and mouth or draw the face with a pencil.

Dolls with pipe-cleaner frames

Basic model

Materials
Pipe-cleaners
Unvarnished wooden beads with a diameter of
  ½" and ¼" (12 and 5 mm).
Pieces of felt
Unspun wool
Thin yellow wool

Method
Double over a pipe-cleaner and glue the folded
end into the hole of the ½" (12 mm) bead to
make a head (Figure 36a). Now twist a second
pipe-cleaner horizontally round the neck of the
first to create arms (Figure 36b). Then cut the
arms and legs off to the right length.

Now start with the trousers. Cut out the legs
from a double piece of felt. The trouser-legs
should reach up to the armpits. Fold them over
the legs and sew them up, securing the top
parts together to form the top of the trousers.

Cut out the smock as in the pattern in Figure
37 and lay it round the doll's shoulders. Sew
up the arms and the back. You can give the
doll a different coloured strip of felt round the
neck.

Glue unspun wool or some single strands of
yarn onto the head for hair.

If you wish cut out the gnome's cap in Figure 37 and sew it up the back before sticking
it to the head.

The dolls are about 2¼" (6 cm) high.

A girl
The girl in Figure 38 has a dress instead of a
smock (see the pattern in Figure 37). Her hair
is made from a thin woollen strand. Wind it at
least ten times round four fingers. Take it off
the fingers and sew these twenty (or so) strands
together by taking another strand of wool and
threading it through the middle of the hair
several times.

Then glue the hair onto the head. Once the
glue is dry trim the hair to the correct shape.

Figure 36.

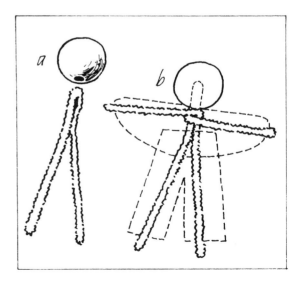

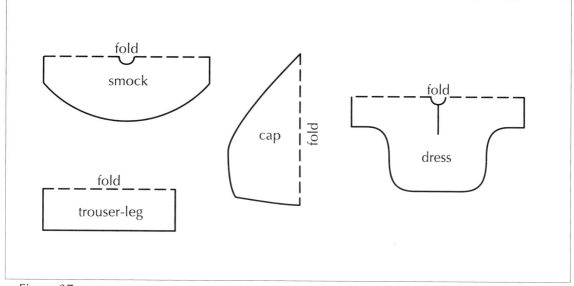

fold

smock

cap

fold

fold

dress

fold

trouser-leg

∧ *Figure 37.*

∨ *Figure 38.*

35

A Christmas gnome

Materials
A long pipe-cleaner or thin wire
Plain varnished bead, diameter ½" (12 mm)
Four red beads, diameter ¼" (5 mm)
Unspun wool or carded fleece
Pieces of felt
Glue

Method
The gnome shown in Figure 39 is about 2¼" (6 cm) tall.

If you do not have pipe-cleaners you can use thin wire to make the frame instead.

Cut off a piece of pipe-cleaner or wire 20"–24" (50–60 cm) long. Push it through the plain varnished bead which becomes the head.

Make sure that the bead is in the middle of the wire with the hole lying vertically. Twist the two ends of the wire together to make a neck of about ¼" (5 mm) (Figure 40a).

Now bend the wires out left and right and run a red bead onto each wire. Bend each wire round its bead, bringing the end back to the neck. Twist the wire together, thus making an arm and a hand (length 1", 2.5 cm). The wires now cross at the neck (Figure 40b).

Bring the two wires downwards. Now thread a wire through them 1½" (4 cm) below the neck to make the legs. Bend the wire back in the same way as for the arms. Finally twist the two leg-wires together up to the armpits. Do this for each leg (Figure 40c).

The frame is now finished. Wrap some thin teased wool or carded fleece round it.

Cut out the pattern in Figure 41 and drape the suit (which is like a boiler-suit) round the doll. Trim if necessary. Sew up the trouser-legs and then the arms and finally the back of the suit.

Cut out the cap, sew up the back and glue it to the head. Finally cut out the collar and sew it on.

This gnome can sit on the branch of a Christmas tree. If you wish, you can make it a little bigger.

Figure 39.

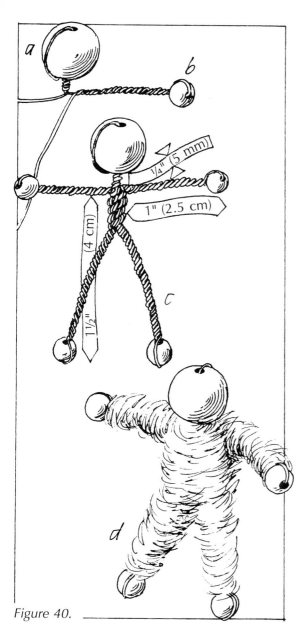

Figure 40.

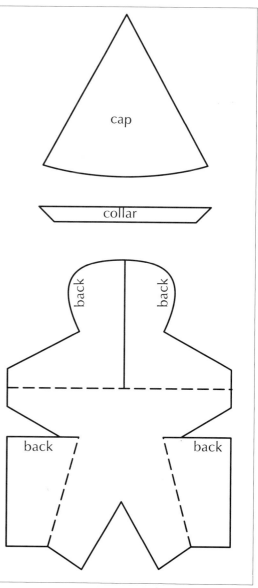

Figure 41. Pattern for Christmas gnome.

37

Jester

Materials
Pipe-cleaner or wire
Unvarnished wooden bead with a diameter of
    $5/8$" (16 mm)
Unspun wool
Pieces of felt
Little bell

Method
See pages 36f for instructions on how to make the pipe-cleaner frame. Wrap some thinly teased unspun wool loosely round the frame.

The dark-red jester in Figure 43 has a suit which consists of a left and a right half of the same colour (see the pattern in Figure 42b). Cut out the pattern of the suit twice using two layers of felt. Open out the felt and lay the wrapped round frame between the two layers, the front and back. Sew the two halves of the suit together, taking care to use small stitches. The jester's *hands* and *feet* are attached to the rest of the suit. Tie up the hands at the wrists, and the feet at the ankles.

Cut out the *collar* in Figure 42a, gather it, lay it round the neck and sew the collar onto the jester's back. Cut out the *jester's cap* from a double piece of felt, sew it together and glue it onto the head. You can attach a little bell or a coloured bead onto the conical cap.

The dolls illustrated are about 3" (7–8 cm) high without caps.

Variation
Instead of the jester's one-piece suit you can make a suit, collar and cap out of two halves of different colours. This time cut out the felt, one piece at a time, and first sew the two halves of the different colours together so that you get a front and a back. Finish off the jester as before.

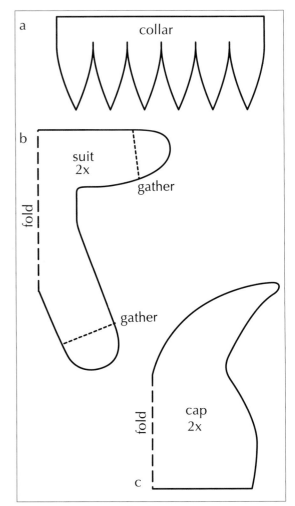

Figure 42. Pattern for jester.

Figure 43.

Man made with pipe-cleaners

Materials
Pipe-cleaners
Unvarnished wooden bead with a diameter of
    ½" (12 mm)
Pink knitted cotton
Pieces of felt
Little red beads

Method
Begin in the same way as for the *basic model*
(page 34, Figure 36), but use a longer piece
of pipe-cleaner. This is because this time the
pipe-cleaner is not cut off but bent round for
the arms and legs, so that they are made out
of a double pipe-cleaner (Figure 45a). If the

Figure 44.

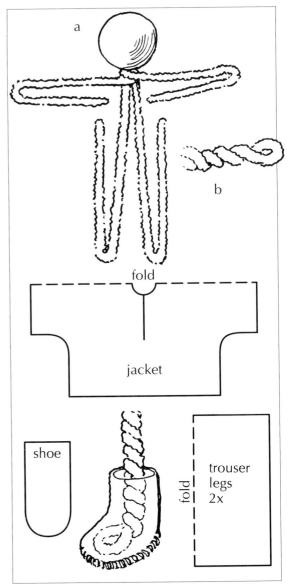

Figure 45. Pattern for pipe-cleaner man.

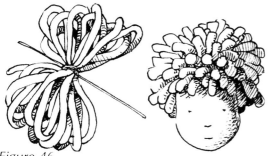

Figure 46.

pipe-cleaner is too long wind the excess round the body.

Clothe the hands with a small piece of pink knitted cotton and secure this at the wrists.

The pattern in Figure 45 consists of a jacket, two trouser-legs and two shoes.

First make the shoes by sewing the two pieces of felt together, pulling them up over the feet and tying them on.

Take the two trouser-legs, fold them round the legs and sew them up. They should reach up to the armpits. Sew the tops of the trouser-legs together to make a pair of trousers.

Cut out the jacket making sure that the neck-opening is big enough to push the head through. Sew up the front of the jacket and attach the beads.

Sew the hair on the middle of the head only. After cutting the loops you can glue the hair onto the head in locks (Figure 46).

The doll is about 3½" (9 cm) long.

The man in the moon

Materials
Pipe-cleaners
Unvarnished bead with ⁵⁄₈" (16 mm) diameter
Pieces of felt
Unspun wool
Small red beads with a diameter of ¹⁄₈" (4 mm)
An iron ring with a diameter of 3½" (8–9 cm), or a piece of cane

Method
See pages 36f for instructions on how to make the basic form. Thinly teased wool is then wound round the frame for the man in the moon, as was the case with the *Christmas gnome*.

Figure 47.

Sew the trousers firmly onto the man (see the pattern in Figure 48). Gather the trouser-leg in at the foot, draw in the thread and secure it before attaching the beads to the material to make the feet.

Cut open the jacket at the back and sew it firmly onto the doll. Gather in the ends of the sleeves and attach the small beads for hands (Figure 47).

Give the man some unspun wool for hair.

Without his cap the gnome is 2½" (6 cm) tall. To make the cap, cut out the material using the pattern, sew it up at the back and glue it onto the head.

Take the iron ring or make a ring of cane and wind yellow wool round it. Lay the ring on a piece of felt so that you can draw a crescent moon which you then cut out, and sew onto the ring. Tie a golden thread to the ring and hang it up.

Figure 48. Pattern for man in the moon.

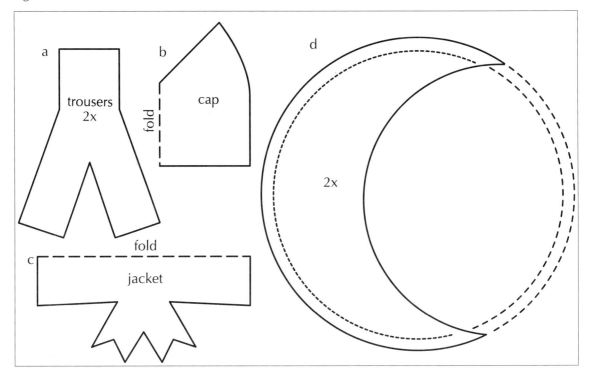

Wooden doll with moveable arms and legs

Materials
A wooden doll (see *Method*)
Pieces of felt
Knitting wool for the hair

Method
In craft shops you can buy dolls which have wooden heads, bodies, hands and feet, but whose arms and legs are made of wire wrapped in cord. These dolls can stand with

their arms and legs bent in various postures (Figure 50). Dolls made with pipe-cleaners can be shaped into various postures but they are usually unable to stand.

Begin by dressing the feet. Glue a piece of felt onto the sole of the foot and trim round each foot leaving a margin of about $^1/_{16}$" (1–2 mm). Cut out the tops of the shoes following the pattern in Figure 49c and glue these onto the feet

Figure 49. Pattern for wooden doll.

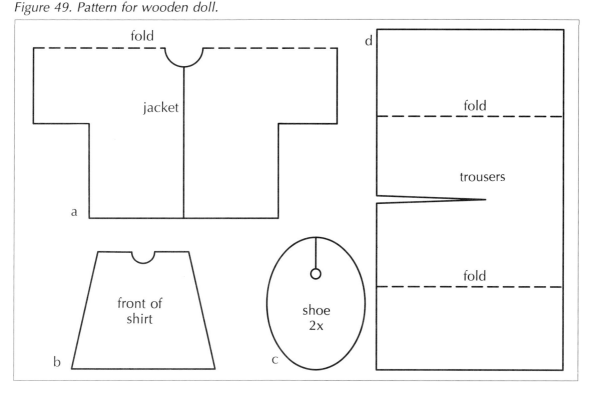

too. Trim off the surplus felt and sew the tops to the felt soles.

Cut out the trousers as in the pattern in Figure 49d and sew them onto the back of the doll. If necessary slant both ends in slightly at the waist. The trousers should reach almost up to the armpits.

Because the doll has a jacket he only needs the front of a shirt (Figure 49b). Sew the top of the shirt around the neck with a few stitches and sew the bottom onto the trousers.

Finally cut out the jacket as in Figure 49a. sew up the seams and put it on the doll.

See page 8 for the hair.

Figure 50.

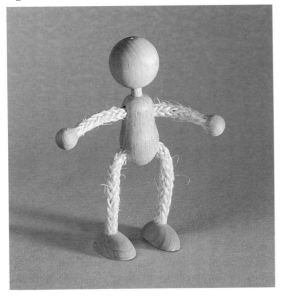

Animals and Birds

Duck

Materials
Felt
Thin card
Unspun wool

Method
The pattern in Figure 52 has two similar sides, two wings, the base, the beak and the eyes.

Follow the pattern to cut out the base parts from pieces of felt.

Use a piece of card for the base so that the bird will stand.

Sew up the head and neck making sure that the beak is secured between both sides of the head. Before sewing up the rest of the body fill the head and neck with some unspun wool. Keep stuffing the body as you go on sewing it up. Leave the underside half-open and sew it up only when the body is fully stuffed.

Figure 51.

Take the wings and sew them onto the front of the body.

Cut out a small circle for the eye and sew it on in the right place. If you prefer you can embroider the eyes.

The ducks shown are 2"–2¼" (5–6 cm) wide (Figure 51).

Figure 52. Pattern for ducks.

Swan

Materials
Felt
Thin card
Unspun wool
Red embroidery thread

Method
Unlike the *duck* for which the head, neck and body are one piece with the wings sewn onto

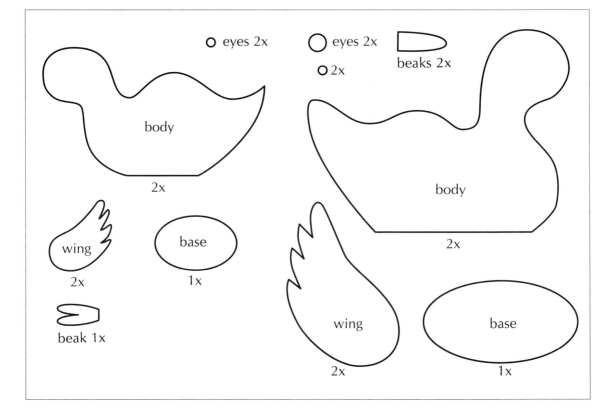

the body, the swan consists of three parts: firstly the head, neck and wings, secondly the rest of the body, and thirdly the base. Cut out the base following the pattern in Figure 53 plus a little piece of card to stabilize it.

First sew the head and neck together and fill them with unspun wool.

Then partly sew up the body, leaving an opening large enough to stuff the wool into the body.

Once the body is fully stuffed sew it up. Insert the piece of card at the base and sew it in, as for the *duck.*

Now bring the wings (with neck and head attached) over the body and secure them to the underside of the body. Sew two small circles of felt onto the head for eyes, or embroider them. Embroider the beak in the same way.

The swan is about 3¼" (8 cm) wide and 3¼" (8 cm) high.

Figure 53. Pattern for swan.

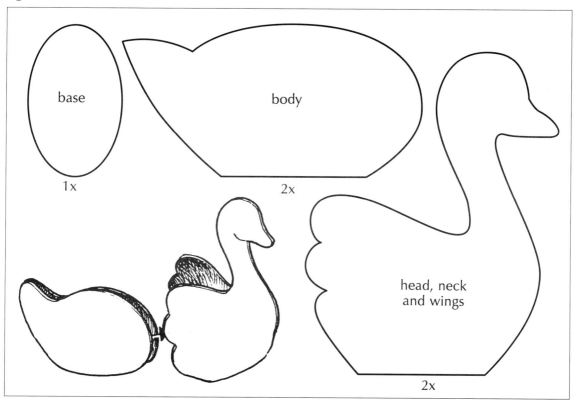

base
1x

body
2x

head, neck
and wings
2x

Seal

Materials
Pieces of felt
Unspun wool
Beads

Method
The pattern in Figure 55 has one piece for the head, the body and the flippers, and one piece for the belly and the flippers. There is also an inset piece for the head.

Cut out the pattern and sew together the two belly pieces which together make the underside of the body.

First sew the inset piece of the head to one of the sides and then join both side-pieces (with the inset piece) together half way down the back, leaving the rest of the back open.

Now lay the two pieces which make up the belly inside the rest of the body with the edge inwards. Sew the breast, the front flippers, the sides and the hind flippers together in that order. Stuff the seal and then sew up the back.

To finish off you can use red beads for the eyes, and embroider on some whiskers (Figure 54).

Figure 55. Pattern for seal.

Figure 54.

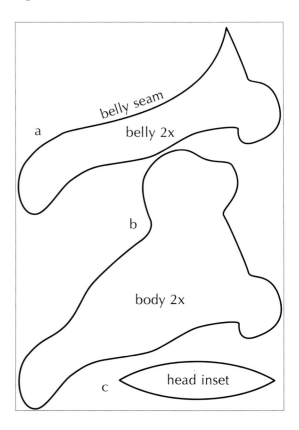

Bird

Materials
Piece of felt
Unspun wool
Pipe-cleaner

Method
The pattern in Figure 56 has three pieces: the upper part of the body with the wings, a separate piece for the wings, and two separate side pieces for the head and body.

Sew the detached wings to the underside of the body with the wings. The material for the wings is now double so it should be quite firm. Despite this the wings will soon hang down a little. If you do not want them to do this, either sew in a pipe-cleaner along the front of the wings or insert a thin piece of card between them.

Now take the two sides of the head and body and sew them together at the bottom. The two sides now make the beak, head, body and tail. Sew them onto the top of the body. Leave a little bit at the tail open for stuffing the body

Figure 56. Pattern for bird.

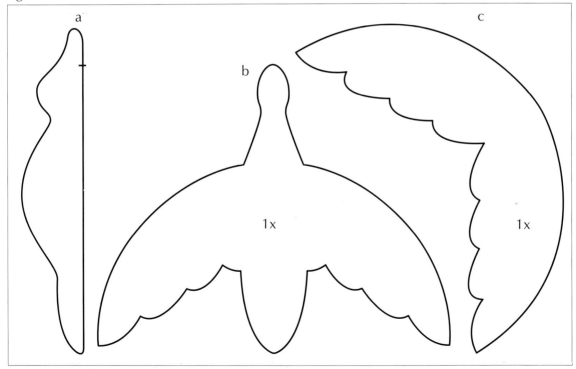

Figure 57.

with unspun wool. This ensures that the wings are not stuffed.

Sew up the body and embroider the eyes. Use orange or red embroidery thread for the beak. Embroider the end of the beak first so that you can then wind the thread round the beak and fasten it off.

Pass a thread right through the body so that the bird can fly (hang). Before fastening off make sure that it is hangs effectively.

Variation

Birds are suitable for using in mobiles. This can consist of a hoop on which a number of birds are hung, but it can also be a more intricate mobile consisting of a number of separate rods.

You can add variety by varying the size and colour of the birds.

Mobile with butterflies·

Materials
Pieces of felt
Pipe-cleaners
Thin green wire
Small beads

Method
The butterflies have wings made of two layers of felt glued together and sewn together round the edge if necessary.

Figure 59 shows how you can use your imagination to vary the shape of the wings and also the shapes cut into the wings. It is fun to choose attractive colour combinations for the

Figure 58. Pattern for butterfly wings.

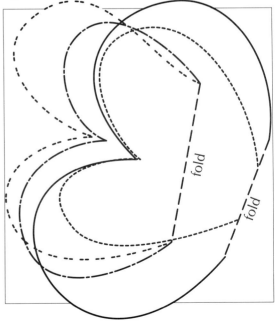
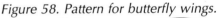

Figure 59.

different layers of felt which are revealed by the shapes cut into the wings.

The inside of the body consists of a piece of pipe-cleaner about 2" (5 cm) long. Make two antennae about ¾" (2 cm) long from a piece of thin (green) wire. Thread a bead onto each end of this and wind the ends of the wire back round the beads. Bend the ends of the pipe-cleaner and attach the middle to make two antennae.

Now clothe the pipe-cleaner with a narrow strip of brown felt about 2¼" x ½" (6 x 1.5 cm). Then wind coloured thread or woollen yarn around the body. The gap between the threads should be about ¼" (5 mm). Sew the wings onto the body.

Hanging up the butterflies — as for example on a round hoop wrapped in wool — requires some care. The butterflies in Figure 59 are hung by making a square out of thin wire. Two opposite sides of the square are the sewn onto the butterfly, one side onto each wing. Two threads can then attach the square of wire to the hoop above. The square of wire can be bent to allow the butterfly to hang well, the wire keeping the wings open (Figure 60).

Snail

Materials
Piece of felt
Unspun wool
Long pipe-cleaner or thin wire
Thin card

Method
The pattern in Figure 61 consists of the snail's body, shell and two horns. The body consists of a base and the two sides, all as one piece.

It is essential to stick a piece of card at the base of the body, otherwise the snail will fall over with its top-heavy shell. Sew up the snail, leaving a small opening for stuffing in the unspun wool.

Take a long strip of felt tapered along one side for the shell (Figure 61). You will also need a pipe-cleaner about 8" (20 cm) long or two pipe-cleaners joined together. Alternatively, you can use a piece of wire with the ends bent round.

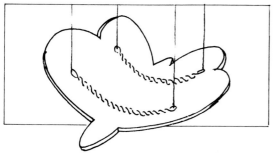

Figure 60.

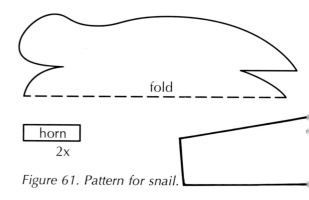

fold

horn
2x

Figure 61. Pattern for snail.

The coil of the shell has to be thicker at the bottom than at the top. You must therefore wind the unspun wool round the pipe-cleaner more thickly at what is to be the bottom end, thinning it out gradually towards the other end. Make sure the felt fits round tightly and sew it on securely.

Now wind the whole tube round to make the shell (Figure 63). Sew the coils together and sew the shell onto the body.

Cut out two small pieces of felt for the *horns,* curl them up firmly, secure them with a few stitches and then sew them onto the head.

∧ *Figure 62.*   ∨ *Figure 63.*

snail's shell 8" (20 cm) long

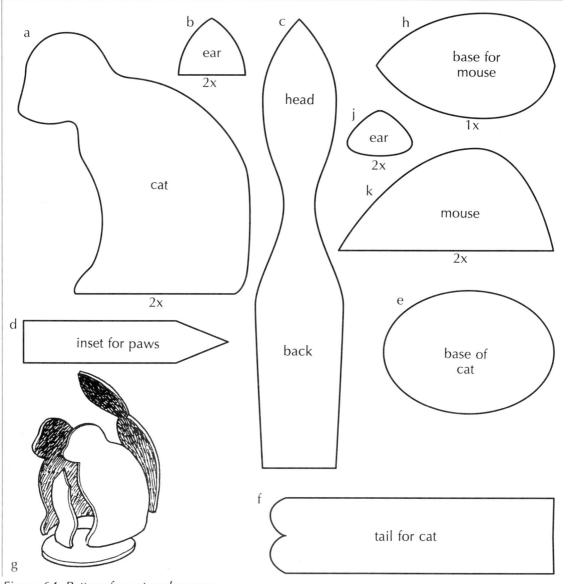

a

b
ear
2x

c
head

h
base for
mouse
1x

j
ear
2x

k
mouse
2x

cat
2x

d
inset for paws

e
base of
cat

back

g

f
tail for cat

Figure 64. Pattern for cat and mouse.

Sitting cat

Materials
Pieces of felt
Unspun wool
Pipe-cleaner
A small bell
Thin card

Method
Cut out the eight parts of the pattern in Figure 64a–f. Take the inset piece for the head and back, and sew the part which is the head between the two side-pieces. Stuff the head with teased wool.

Now go on sewing the body onto the back part, and sew the inset for the paws between the two side-pieces. Stuff the body with teased wool. Cut out a piece of thin card ¹/₁₆" (2 mm) smaller than the felt base and glue this onto the base. Sew the base onto the body.

Now comes the tail. Sew up one of the short sides and the two long sides of the tail and insert a pipe-cleaner before sewing up the last short side. Sew the tail onto the body and the ears onto the head. Embroider the eyes and whiskers. If you wish add a ribbon and a bell.

Mouse

Materials
A piece of felt
Unspun wool
Thin card

Figure 65.

Figure 66.

55

Method

The pattern for the mouse in Figure 64h–j consists of five parts: the body, two sides and two ears. Cut out the pieces and glue a piece of card onto the inside of the body-part. The card should be ¹/₁₆" (2 mm) smaller than the body-part.

Sew the parts together leaving the hind-part slightly open for stuffing. Sew up the opening once the body has been stuffed.

Finish off by sewing on the ears and embroidering the nose and whiskers. Crochet a tail and sew it on.

Dog

Materials
Piece of felt
Unspun wool

Method

Cut out the pattern in Figure 67. It consists of two side-pieces, a belly-piece and an inset piece for the head and two ears.

First sew up the seams of the tail and stuff it with wool. The rest of the body is thus still wide open. Then sew up the back seam of the body, legs, underside and front. Stuff the legs. Secure the inset piece for the head and stuff the head.

Stuff the body and sew up the back.

Cut out the floppy ears and sew them onto the head. The ears can be the same colour as the body or a different colour.

Finish off the dog by embroidering the eyes and nose. If you wish you can give him a collar (Figure 68).

56

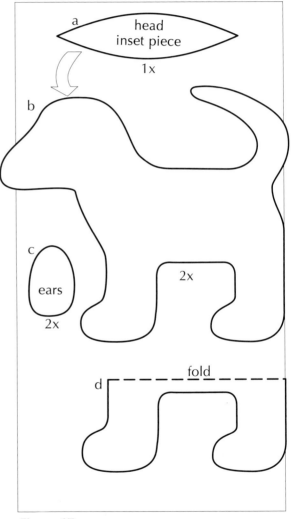

Figure 67.

Figure 68.

Another dog

Materials
Pieces of felt
Unspun wool

Method
The pattern in Figure 70f–j consists of two side-pieces and an inset piece for the head, ears and tail. Cut the pieces out and fold in the insides of the paws. Now trim the soles of the paws, sew them up and fill the legs.

Sew the two parts and the head-inset together, leaving the underside of the body still open for stuffing. Sew up the body after you have stuffed it.

Sew the tail and the two ears onto the dog, and embroider the eyes and the nose.

Horse

Materials
Piece of felt
Unspun wool
Knitting wool

Method
The pattern for the horse (Figure 70a–e) consists of two sides, a belly-piece, the ears and the base of the hooves. In addition the horse has a blanket, a saddle and a girth.

Cut out the parts. Lay the belly-piece between the two side-pieces and sew them together. Sew a hoof base onto each leg and stuff the legs. After that you can sew up the rest of the horse's body leaving a little opening in the back for stuffing. After you have stuffed the body, sew it up.

Now sew on the ears. Embroider the harness and the eyes with some wool and make the mane and tail out of thin wool. Finally, attach a blanket (2¾" x 1½", 7 x 3.5 cm) and a saddle and girth (2½" x ⅜", to the horse's back.

Figure 69.

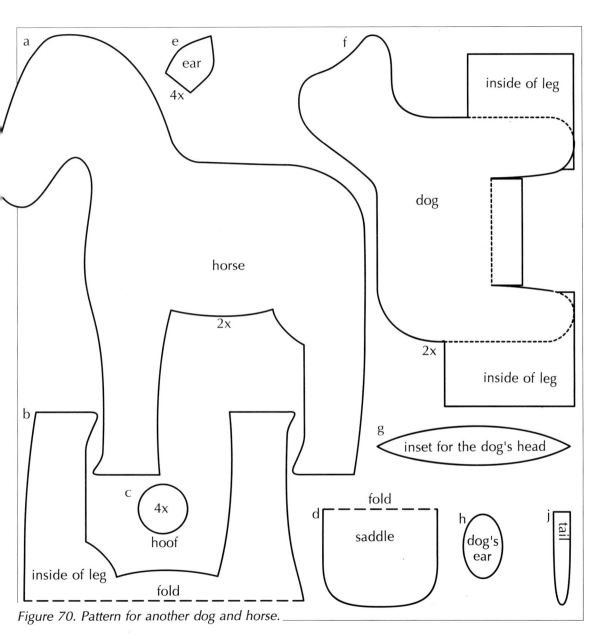

a

e
ear
4x

f

inside of leg

dog

horse

2x

2x

inside of leg

b

g
inset for the dog's head

c
4x
hoof

d
fold
saddle

h
dog's
ear

j
tail

inside of leg
fold

Figure 70. Pattern for another dog and horse.

59

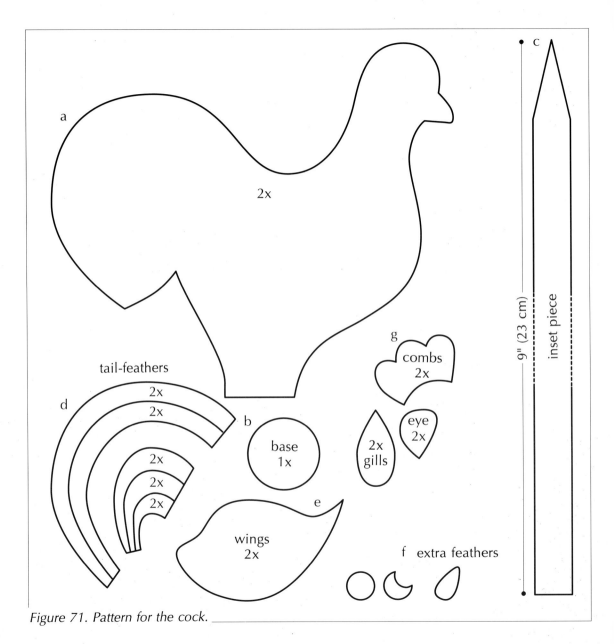

a

2x

c

9" (23 cm)

inset piece

tail-feathers

d

2x

2x

2x

2x

2x

g

combs
2x

b

base
1x

2x
gills

eye
2x

e

wings
2x

f   extra feathers

Figure 71. Pattern for the cock.

Cock

Materials
Piece of felt
Unspun wool
Thin card
Beads

Method

The cock's body consists of four parts: two sides, an inset piece for the top and a base. The other items in Figure 71 are adornments such as the tail-feathers and comb.

Cut out the parts of the pattern. First sew the tail-feathers (Figure 71d) onto the two sides of the cock. Then sew the extra feathers (Figure 71f) onto the wings (Figure 71e), and finally sew the two wings onto the side-pieces.

Sew the brown lower parts of the eyes onto the head (Figure 71g).

To make the body take the two sides and sew the inset piece between them as shown in Figure 73.

Stuff the cock with teased unspun wool and then sew up the front. Finally give him a comb of double felt and two gills (Figure 71g). The eyes are made from beads.

In Figure 72 the cock has a disc of wood to stand on. The felt base (Figure 71b) is glued onto this.

Figure 72.

Figure 73.

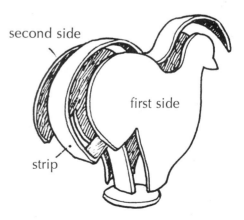

second side

first side

strip

Figure 74.

Tapestries

Simple tapestry

Materials
Pieces of felt
Larger pieces of material

Method
The choice of background for the tapestry will partly depend on the shape and size you have chosen. Pure woollen felt is rather expensive, so for a larger tapestry it is feasible to make the backcloth from another material. For smaller tapestries felt is eminently suitable.

Because felt can be cut and does not fray even very young children can make their own tapestries by sewing the cut-out shapes onto the backcloth.

You can make the tapestry as complicated as you wish. For example, the fish-tapestry shown in Figure 74 is made with fish-shapes sewn onto the backcloth and then the details embroidered on top. The tapestry is 18½" x 17¾" (47 x 45 cm). Although the fish-patterns are given in Figure 75 and 76 you can of course devise your own designs.

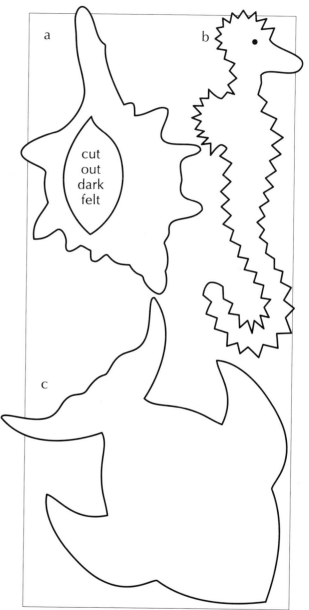

Figure 75.

cut out
dark
felt

Figure 76.

A gnome in a landscape

Materials
Pieces of felt
Strips of wood for the frame
A piece of card
Pipe-cleaners
Unspun wool
Unvarnished wooden beads with a diameter of
    ¾" and ½" (20 and 12 mm)

Method
The dimensions for this tapestry are about 8" x
7" (20 x 18 cm). The gnome (including his
conical hat) is about 5½" (14 cm) tall.

The tapestry of Figure 77 uses a wooden
frame about 1½" deep and ¼" broad (4 x
0.5 cm) instead of just having a backcloth onto
which everything is sewn. All sorts of things,
such as a landscape, water, a house or the
inside of a room and so on, can still be sewn
or embroidered onto the backcloth. The advan-
tage of having a wooden frame is that you can
add three-dimensional figures in front of a
background, such as a gnome, a cat, a snail
and so on.

The tapestry shown is very simple with
pieces of felt sewn onto each other. The
embroidery is confined to the tree but it can
also be used for flowers and so on.

For the illustration in this book the tapestry
has been kept fairly small but it can of course
be made much larger.

When the tapestry is finished it should be
stapled immediately onto a wooden frame. If
necessary you can glue it onto a piece of card
first. If you make the tapestry larger you will
have to use thicker strips of wood.

Figure 77.

The gnome

The gnome is 4" (10 cm) tall without his conical hat. His frame is made in the same way as the pipe-cleaner doll on page 34, but this time the arms and legs are enclosed in a piece of felt (Figure 78). The pieces of felt are the same length as the arms or legs (up to the armpits) and about 3¼" (8 cm) wide. Wrap the pieces of felt round with the ends at the back of the doll. Secure these ends onto the back.

Sew the sleeves and trouser-legs together so that they sit firmly and make a sort of body. Any resulting unevenness will be covered up when the gnome is dressed.

Cut out the smock in Figure 78 and pull it over the neck. Gather the felt in at the waist and finish off by giving the gnome a belt secured at the back.

Give the gnome a beard and hair from unspun wool and glue them onto the head and face. Cut out the hat, sew it up at the back and glue it to the head.

A first book

Materials
Pieces of felt
Cotton material

Method
It is a very good idea if a young child's first book is made of cloth rather than paper or cardboard. This means it is nice and soft and cannot hurt the child.

Because small children are inclined to put everything into their mouth it is important that all the pieces are well sewn on.

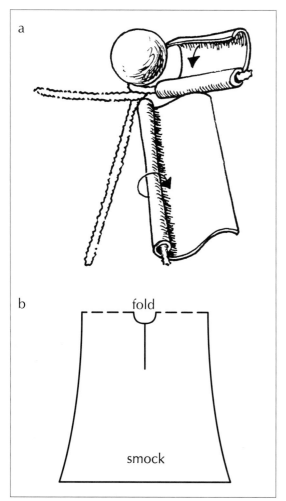

a

b

fold

smock

Figure 78. Pattern for the gnome.

66

Figure 79.

First determine the size of the book and the number of pages. A book for a very small child does not need to have very many pages. In fact eight or ten pages — that is to say four or five opened-out leaves — is quite a lot as children enjoy looking at the same picture over and over again. Keep the pictures as simple and recognizable as possible.

Because pure woollen felt is fairly expensive the little book in Figure 79 is made from cotton material. The pictures can still be made of felt.

Cut out a strip of the material to the intended height of the book and fold the material concertina-wise to make the pages.

Unfold the material again and mark the outline of the pages with a pencil or tacking thread.

Now cut out the felt figures and sew them into position on the pages and finish them off with embroidery if necessary.

Fold the strip back into pages again and sew them together. All the pages should now be sewn together at the spine and attached to the cover.

Because only very simple pictures are required for this book, no patterns have been included.

French knitting

Children from about six years onwards love to do French knitting (also called frame knitting) and finger-crochet with woollen yarn. These are excellent hobbies which each child can do at their own pace.

Materials
Knitting wool
Wooden knitting Nancy or bobbin
Thick darning needle

Method
Let the end of the yarn hang through the hole in the centre of the knitting Nancy or bobbin and twist it loosely round the first peg or staple (Figure 80a). Now go across the middle of the knitting Nancy to the peg on the left-hand side (Figure 80b) and twist the yarn loosely round it. Do the same with the next peg and the final one on the right-hand side (Figure 80c). Now bring the yarn back to the first peg (Figure 80d).

Now take the loop over the yarn and the peg using the needle (Figure 80e).

From now on always twist the yarn clockwise round the pegs so that the last loop can be taken round the yarn and the peg. In this way you make a cord in the hole of the knitting Nancy. In order to achieve an even cord it is important to give the yarn hanging from the knitting Nancy a gentle pull from time to time.

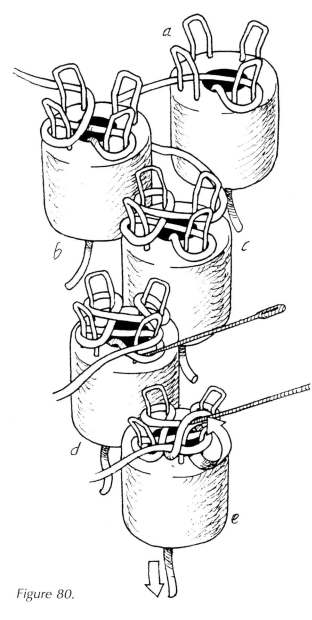

Figure 80.

Finger-crochet

Materials
Thick knitting wool

Method
Make a loop with the knitting wool as shown in Figure 81a and hold the two strands with one hand where they cross.

With your other hand pull the yarn through the loop (Figure 81b) and pull gently. Turn the loop over so that the yarn from the ball now

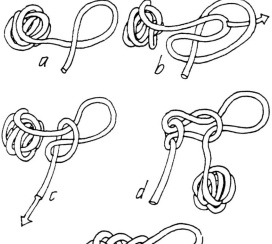

Figure 81.

sits *behind* the loop. Pull this through the loop again and now pull the loop tight (Figure 81c).

Continue in this way until you have produced the pattern in Figures 81d and e.

Once the crocheted chain is long enough, cut off the yarn, pull the end through the loop and tighten.

You can make many things with this crocheted chain. Or it can be used for decoration, as in Figure 82 where the sun is made by winding the chain round and round like the shell of a snail. The decoration on the little bag of Figure 83 is also finger-crochet.

Tapestry with French knitting

Materials
Pieces of felt
Knitting wool
Wooden knitting Nancy or bobbin
A thick needle

Method
This tapestry is also suitable for children to make, but it may be necessary to help them a bit with the sewing up.

Cut out the back-cloth of the tapestry and the designs for it. Let the child make an edging with French knitting allowing them to choose the colours. The house in Figure 82 is also made from a French-knitted cord while the circle for the sun is finger-crocheted.

Figure 82. Tapestry 12" x 6" (30 x 15 cm).

Bag with French-knitted strap

Materials
Piece of felt
Thick knitting wool
Wooden knitting Nancy or bobbin
Thick needle

Method
Take a piece of felt 7" x 4" (18 x 10 cm) and
fold it in two.

Make a design from a finger-crocheted chain
and sew it onto one half of the piece of felt for
decoration.

Then sew up the two sides and attach the
French-knitted cord onto each side.

Figure 83.

Fir-trees and grasses

Materials
Pieces of felt
A little strip of wood
A slice of wood from a log or stick

Method
The trees described here can make a very
attractive background for the dolls and animals
described earlier.

Saw a little strip of wood which is at least
½" (1.5 cm) shorter than the felt tree onto
which it will be glued. Fix the strip of wood
onto a thin base of wood to make a stand for
the tree. The size of the base depends on the
size of the tree.

The effect of grass can be created by making
cuts into one side of a narrow strip of felt and
then gluing this to a piece of wood so that it
will stand up (Figure 51).

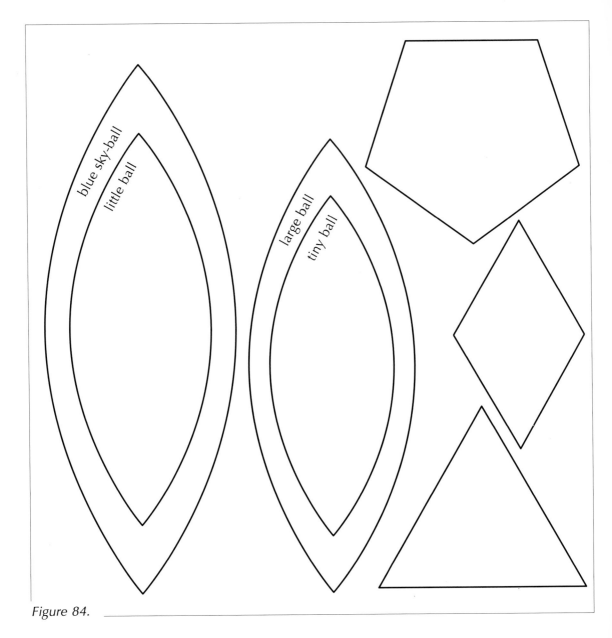

Figure 84.

Balls

The balls described in this book are made in various ways. The most commonly used consists of six sections. There are other types described, one is made up of twelve pentagons, another of twenty triangles, and another of ten diamonds.

Materials
Pieces of felt
Unspun wool
Embroidery thread

Method
Figure 84 shows the patterns for the various balls. Cut out the required number of parts (see above) and sew them together with small stitches.

Figure 85 shows how different kinds of stitches can be used for sewing up the balls. If you wish you can use embroidery thread of the same colour as the felt so that the stitches will hardly show. On the other hand you can deliberately take a contrasting colour so that the result adds decoration. Pages 6 and 7 show various suitable stitches.

Felt can pull apart, so it is advisable to tack the separate pieces of felt together first before sewing the whole ball together.

Leave a piece of felt open before sewing up the ball completely, so that you can stuff the ball with teased unspun wool. Finally sew up the last piece.

You can obtain endless variations by using different colours. You can also make a plain ball and embellish it by embroidering it, or by sewing on a felt design. This is the procedure with the blue sky-ball, on the one side of which is the sun, and on the other the moon and the stars.

Figure 85.

Trinkets

Necklaces and earrings

Materials
Pieces of felt
Wire
Chain lockets
Various die-cuts
Earring hooks or clamps
Beads

Method
Making a necklace is an excellent pastime for a rainy afternoon and children can make them themselves. Little scraps of felt can be used.

Pennon necklace
The pattern in Figure 86 shows little pennons of various kinds, which are used as the basis. By varying the sizes and shapes of these you can make the necklaces more imaginative.

Cut out the required number of pennons. Roll them round a skewer and sew up the point. Pull out the skewer and thread the knot you have formed onto a thread. Continue in the same way. Once the necklace is long enough attach a locket and catch to each end.

Rolled felt and bead necklace
Oblong pieces of felt make quite a different effect from that of the rolled round pennons (Figure 87, second from right). Otherwise the method is the same.

Unlike the former necklace you now thread real beads between the felt beads.

Scrap felt and bead necklace
For this necklace you only need scraps. Cut out little squares of various sizes from the scraps. Thread one square scrap and one bead alternately onto the wire until you have obtained the required length of necklace (Figure 87, left). Naturally you can use any shape you wish for this necklace, and do not have to be restricted to squares.

Figure 86.

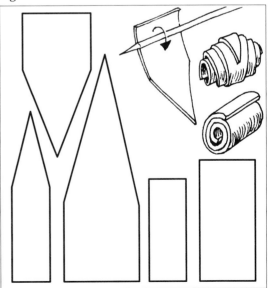

Figure 87. Neclaces from left: round disc, (earrings); scrap felt; rolled felt; pennon.

Round disc necklace

With little round discs of felt you can make endless variations of very beautiful necklaces. As it would take a very long time to cut out so many discs you can use small die-cuts or hollow punches.

To do this lay a piece of felt on a wooden board and bash out the discs with a punch and hammer. The red necklace in Figure 87 has discs of ¼", ⁵/₁₆", ³/₈" and ½" (6, 8, 10 and 12 mm). Thread a little bead between each disc. In the necklace shown two discs of the same size are threaded together, so two discs of ¼" (6 mm), two of ⁵/₁₆" (8 mm), two of ³/₈" (10 mm), and two of ½" (12 mm). After that the discs become smaller again. Thus for each colour group fourteen discs are used. Of course this can be varied. In the necklace in Figure 87 the colours are placed symmetrically; that is to say, the colour groups advancing from either side of the locket are always the same and only the very middle has a different colour.

Earrings

Follow the same principle to make matching earrings. In the earrings shown, all the colours used in the round disc necklace have been included in two groups, but you can of course make the earrings in one colour.

Figure 88.

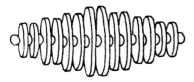

Advancing from the earring hook, thread one group of discs. Finish this off with an extra felt disc and two beads before threading the second group and coming back round to the hook (Figures 87 and 88).

Harlequin brooch

Materials
Pieces of felt
A large bead with a diameter of ⁵/₈" (15 mm)
Three beads with a diameter of ³/₁₆" (5 mm)
Two beads with a diameter of ¼" (7 mm)
Small beads
Thick coloured sewing-thread
Safety-pin

Method
The harlequin in Figures 89 and 90 consists of round and oval discs of felt threaded together with a small bead between. The oval discs are about twice as wide as the round ones.

Choose the colour and cut out or punch out the round and oval discs.

The harlequin is made up of:
— 8 oval discs, 1" (25 mm) wide for the body,
— 10 round discs for each leg, ⁹/₁₆" (14 mm),
— 8 round discs for each arm, ½" (12 mm).

Begin with the legs. Lay out the round discs in the desired order. Take a thread at least 12" (30 cm) long and thread on a ¼" (7 mm) bead. The bead makes the foot. Bring the two ends of the thread together, and thread them through the eye of a needle. Now thread the first of the ⁹/₁₆" (14 mm) round discs onto the needle, followed by a bead, and then another round disc. Continue until you have threaded ten round discs and ten beads.

Put this first leg to one side with the needle still on it and repeat for the second leg.

Now take the first oval disc and bring the two threads of each leg through it, the threads from the left leg slightly to the left and the threads from the right leg slightly to the right of the centre of the disc. Then thread each pair of threads through a bead, and so on. When you come to the last oval but one bring the threads more towards the middle of the oval, and even more so with the last oval (Figure 90).

Make the arms in the same way as the legs, but use the $^{3}/_{16}$" (5 mm) beads for the hands. The arms have two round discs then two beads in succession threaded upwards. Join the arms to the last but one oval of the body. Pass the thread through the middle of the last oval.

Now pass the threads of the arms and legs through the large bead (the head). Because the hole in this bead is quite big fasten the threads on top of the head by threading on a smaller bead and then tying up all the loose ends.

The harlequin still needs his conical hat. Take a strip of felt 2" x 1½" (5 x 4 cm) and glue it onto the head. Trim it and sew it on at the back. The threads on which the whole harlequin has been threaded can be left sticking out of the conical hat as a brush, but they will have to be secured with a few stitches.

Now sew the topmost discs of the arms to the back of the last oval. The arms will then hang well against the body.

Finally attach a safety-pin to the conical hat and to the back of the oval discs to complete the brooch.

Figure 89.

Figure 90.

Clown brooch

Materials
Pieces of felt
White bead
Red beads
Safety-pin
Thin wire

Method
The head and arms of this clown are made with thin wire in the same way as the Christmas gnome on page 36 (Figure 40), but this time the frame is not brought down towards the lower body.

The pattern in Figure 91a–e consists of a jacket, a pair of trousers with feet and a cap. Cut out the jacket and make a cut in the back at the same time so that it can be laid round the upper body and sewn up. Cut out the trousers and sew the two parts together with the blanket-stitch, time sewing the feet between the two parts of the trouser-legs at the same. Sew the trousers onto the jacket and gather the waist in a bit. Glue the cap onto the head and embroider the loops round the edge for decoration (Figure 89).

Finally fasten a safety-pin vertically to the trousers.

Gnome brooch

Materials
Pieces of felt
Beads for the head, hands and feet
Thin wire
Safety-pin

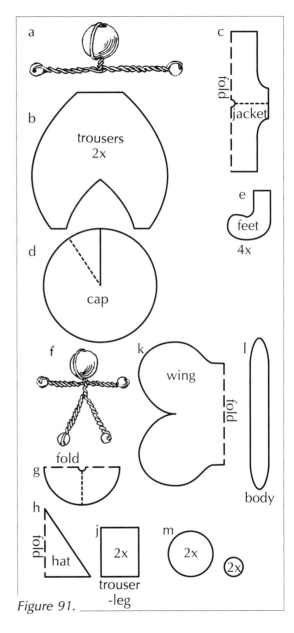

Figure 91.

Method
This gnome is made in the same way as the *Christmas-tree gnome* on page 36, but here the measurements are much smaller and the wire is not wrapped round with wool (Figures 89 and 91f–j).

Cut out the parts of the pattern. Make the frame and sew the trousers round the legs. Cut the back right open and make an opening for the neck. Wrap the smock round the arms and body` and secure it.

Sew up the back seam of the conical hat and glue this onto the head.

Give the gnome a neck-cloth out of a thin strip of yellow felt or woollen yarn. Finally sew a safety-pin onto the back of the gnome.

Butterfly-brooch

Materials
Pieces of felt
Safety-pin

Method
See Figure 91c for the pattern for the butterfly. Cut out the wings and sew the round pieces of felt onto them. Finish off the edges with a decorative stitch, for instance blanket-stitch.

Take two pieces of felt for the body, sew these together and then onto the wings. Finally attach the safety-pin to the underside of the butterfly (Figures 89 and 91k–m).

Figure 92.

Gifts

Doll in a matchbox

Materials
Pieces of felt
Little wooden doll 1¼" (3 cm) high
Matchbox

Method
Cut out a piece of felt to fit exactly over the cover of the matchbox. Decorate the part which will form the matchbox top by embroidering or sewing on a design such as a flower. Now glue the felt round the cover.

Line the inside of the box with white felt.

Take a little wooden doll and dress the body with pink felt, gathering the piece of felt in at the top and bottom. In this way it fits neatly round the neck.

Make the arms out of a piece of felt 1½" x ½" (4 x 1 cm). Fold the two ends and sew them together to make arms, sewing on tiny pieces of felt for the hands at the same time. Sew the middle of the strip onto the doll's back.

For the bonnet take a piece of felt 1" x ⅝" (2.5 x 1.5 cm), fold it in two, sew up the back and sew it onto the body.

Finally insert a small coloured piece of felt into the matchbox as a blanket.

A bookmark

Materials
Pieces of felt

Method
A bookmark is very simple for children to make. Cut out a narrow strip of felt, for example 6½" x 1½" (16 x 4 cm). Decorate it as you wish either by sewing on bits of felt or by embroidering it. You can finish off the sides with a blanket-stitch (Figure 1). You can also sew a thin piece of lining to the back to cover the stitches.

Comb case

Materials
Pieces of felt

Method
Select a suitable comb and then cut out two pieces of felt to measure. Decorate one of the pieces, then sew the two pieces together with an ornamental stitch (Figure 1) leaving the top open.

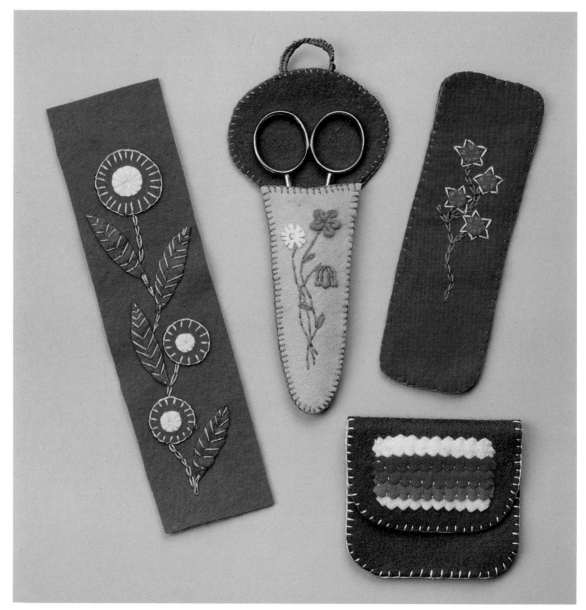

Figure 93.

Scissor case

Materials
Pieces of felt
Thin card

Method
Cut out the back of the case (Figure 93) twice, together with a piece of thin card $1/16''$ (2 mm) smaller than the case.

Place the card between the two pieces of felt and sew these together with invisible stitches.

Now cut out the front and decorate it. Sew the back and front together and finish off the case by working a blanket-stitch round it (Figure 1).

Purse

Materials:
Pieces of felt
Press-studs or buttons

Method:
The pattern for the purse in Figure 95 consists of a piece which forms the back and the flap, the front and a fastening for the flap. Cut out the back and embellish the front-flap. Sew the inside of the flap and the front of the purse with blanket-stitch (Figure 1). Finally attach on or two press-studs.

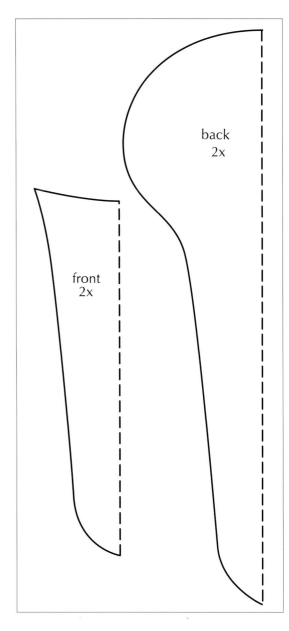

back
2x

front
2x

Figure 94.

83

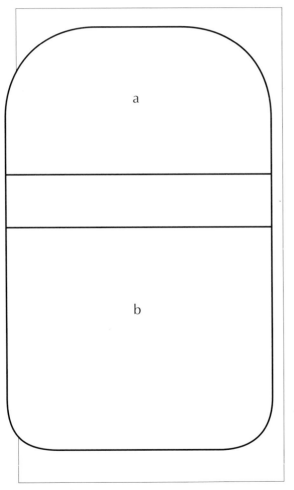

Figure 95.

Decorating little boxes

Materials
Pieces of felt
Boxes

Method
You can obtain wooden boxes of all sizes in craft shops. Choose one and glue some felt all over the outside of the bottom part of the box, leaving the top edge and the top parts of the sides clear so that the lid will fit. Experiment by trying on the lid to see exactly how much space needs to be left clear. Now cut out a piece of felt for the top and decorate it. You can embroider the felt or glue other bits of felt onto it, or you can do a combination of both.

Figure 96.

The rose in Figure 96 consists of two discs cut in towards the middle in four places. Bring the points to the centre and secure them, thus making four petals. Finally sew the two discs with petals together and secure them to the piece of felt with a few stitches. Finally glue the felt onto the lid of the box and trim if necessary.

Egg-cosies

Materials
Pieces of felt
Unspun wool
Embroidery thread
Beads

Egg-cosy with flowers
Figure 99 shows an egg-cosy with flowers. Cut the flowers out from a piece of felt and sew them onto the background. This egg-cosy can be made in many different ways including working simply with embroidery thread on the felt.

Patterned egg-cosy
Cut out the pattern in Figure 98 and embellish one or both sides before sewing them together. You can do this by embroidering something onto them, or by sewing on small cut-out felt flowers.

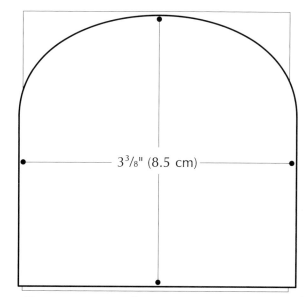

$3^3/_8$" (8.5 cm)

Figure 97. Pattern for egg-cosy with flowers.

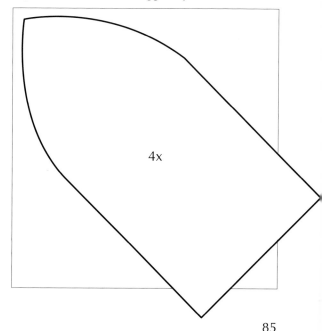

4x

Figure 98. Patterned egg-cosy.

Figure 99.

Hen egg-cosy
Cut out the body from the pattern in Figure 99 twice, the wings twice, the beak twice and the comb once.

Sew the wings onto the body. Then sew the two halves of the hen's body together with button-hole stitch, time sewing the comb between the two parts at the same. Finish off the underside also with button-hole stitch. Sew the two red beaks in position and fill the head with some wool.

Finally sew on two beads for the eyes.

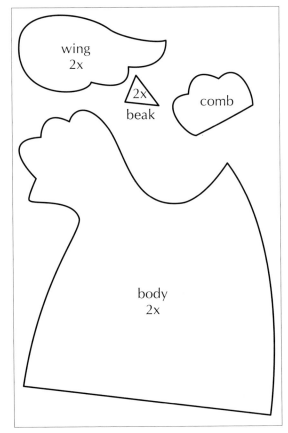

Figure 100.

Materials

Some of the materials used in this book are not easy to find, and may take some time to locate.

Felt
In the Introduction we declared our preference for *pure woollen felt* as against acrylic felt or half-synthetic material as the latter are very thin and the threads are too loosely woven, so while it is being sewn it can easily come apart.

Wooden dolls
Unvarnished wooden dolls with cylindrical or tapered bodies are available in various sizes.

There are also ready-made wooden dolls with moveable arms of wire and cord.

Various materials
Knitted cotton (white, pink and brown).
Teased, unspun wool, or carded fleece.
Cotton material.
Fairy-tale wool is dyed carded fleece. It is not easily obtainable except in Germany and the Netherlands, and you may have to dye your own.

Other items
Pipe-cleaners.
Unvarnished wooden beads are obtainable in several sizes and colours. Those used in this book have a diameter of $^3/_{16}$" $^1/_4$" $^1/_2$" $^5/_8$" $^3/_4$" $1^1/_4$" (5, 7, 12, 16, 20 and 32 mm).
Varnished wooden beads with a diameter of $^1/_8$" $^3/_{16}$" $^1/_4$" (4, 5 and 6 mm).
Necklace-lockets or catches
Earring hooks or clasps
Small bells
Wooden boxes
For *thin card* you can use thick cartridge paper.
Stiff card is 2 or 3-ply board (170–200 gsm).
Glue. A tube with a very thin nozzle is easiest to use.
A knitting Nancy

Ironmongery
Dies or punches $^1/_4$", $^5/_{16}$" $^3/_8$" $^1/_2$" $^9/_{16}$" (6, 8, 10, 12 and 14 mm).
Pinking scissors.
Iron rings with a diameter of about $3^1/_2$" (9 cm).
Thin (copper) wire, thickness $^1/_{32}$" (0.8–1 mm).

Pure woollen felt
Richard Wernekinck

PURE NEW WOOL

Worldwide wholesale trade of the original, classic pure woollen felt; as well as a range of PURE NEW WOOL and woollen products.

Our felt is a top-quality product, made from the finest virgin wools to the International Wool Secretariat standards.
Always certified authentic by a guarantee label showing woolmark, colour number and dye batch number.

Our felt • is sturdier and thicker than ordinary craft felt
• does not shrink or lose shape • does not tear, crease or fray
• is colour-fast and comes in 70 beautiful colours • is ecologically sound
In short, it's fun to work with our pure wollen felt.

For information:
RICHARD WERNEKINCK
Buitenwatersloot 71
2613 TB Delft, Holland   tel.   +31-15-2146341
www.wernekinck.com   fax.   +31-15-2132004

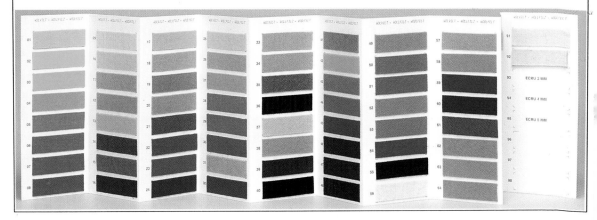